The Eucalypts

Mollie Yang

BookLeaf
Publishing

Presentation by *BookLeaf Publishing*

Web: www.bookleafpub.com

E-mail: info@bookleafpub.com

ISBN: 978-93-95784-38-2

First edition 2022

DEDICATION

the butterfly girl

ACKNOWLEDGEMENT

Thank you to those who read my work and feel something, want to, or need to.

PREFACE

This collection is one of memory, fantastical thought and hope - my brain's gift to the world. It's my thanks to those who love me and my way of saying it back. There are pieces of those who have shown me love in each word I write, so I hope you find yourself inside.

It's Not My Birthday (Fever Dream Beginnings)

A Japanese man walked through the wall
closed it
smoked a cigarette, bird on his head

We watched from the shade in a circle
palms sweating
ashes burning,
until fire hit us through the forehead
eyes closed, breath slow

It got darker
The fairy boy ran with an open umbrella, raising wind
it tasted like wine and socialising
without the obligation of first dates

The ladies had cucumbers on their foreheads
but seemed not to notice
they took turns whipping cream with their hands
passing the bowl until it turned to butter
Massaged oil into each other, touching scalps, soft and slow
like it wasn't intimate

We watched the fairy lights move throw creeping shadow
and time pass
like we were onlookers to something private
we were never meant to see

Tsunami (Author Introduction)

My goal is to live
in the quiet and powerful moments I bring myself

To thank my body for carrying strength
so carefully in my bones,
and throwing it like grenades when needed,
but all the while
keeping heart and fingertips full of warm soft love

To stand up tall and remember
I am quiet and calm
and true and loud,
and that my actions are tsunamis
that only coat the earth with water
to feed the plants

Trees

3

There's this concept of love I met once

It felt like

Being high in the trees
A tropical heat, a breeze
You tuning a guitar and bread baking
As we hummed and touched hands

We watched your parents laughing through the
window
As I lay on my back on the wood

And it felt still and silent
Watching you breathe and frown a little
You focussing on what you love
Me watching your chest fall
A timber bed, soft as silk

Feeling entirely whole and empty

Snapshot (The Butterfly Girl)

Burnt butter in a casserole dish
A bottle of whiskey on paperbacks
Blue paint dried paintbrush near the sink

White sheets on the clothesline swaying
There's a yellow sock in the dirt

Someone's digging a hole next door
They're scraping the shovel on concrete

Pill bottles lined up like soldiers near the window
Six of them no lids
One missing

Her

She's playing with a camera
An instant one
It clicks

A frame of the cat on the windowsill captured
Watch it print

Brow crease
She pulls it out and waves it in the air
Fingertips careful
Shows me
It hasn't developed yet

That strawberry blonde light

What do I think
I tell her to wait
To keep waving, be patient

The sun hits her
She smiles
I hold it in my heart

Waves

I miss you in tiny waves in my belly
Underground tides hit shore now and again
My ocean's off centre
Under the Earth there are explosions
You're too far away to feel

Work (On Loss and Connection)

7

An old man, calm and still,
came to me softly and said
he was sorry they were still young
that even though there was distance
it's never easy
and though we weren't close
i saw his heart
and understood what it was for the first time at work

it beat in time and it was large and loud
and as he sat at his desk
humming away
i felt it like he was bursting
yelling from the rooftops so only i could hear

Forehead (Birthing Ideas Like Larvae)

He sits with a deep frown that creases his freckles.
In the centre of the crease lies a small blowfly.
In the blowfly lies a small bacteria.
In the bacteria lies a small secret.
They all rest in the freckles of a frown.

The blowfly that lives in the centre of the crease of
the deep frown lays eggs of knowledge at the centre
of the crevice.
The knowledge sits dormant, waiting.
The blowfly flies away.

He sits with knowledge in the crevice of his deep
frown, where a blowfly once sat.
The knowledge seeps into the skin like honey,
coating his brain in an excellent idea.
He gets up, delighted.
He's had an excellent idea.

The blowfly flies away, carrying a small bacteria.
The bacteria has the power to change the world.
It lies dormant in the stomach of the blowfly.
It sits dormant, waiting

Acid

I tripped acid and thought of you

All of the sadness in my brain
The bits I'm afraid of
Poured out of me like beams of light
And painted the skies
Swirls of blue and indigo
You in blotches

I watched them on my back
Saw them float by like clouds
And coat me like rain
And I drowned in myself
In the blues you gave me
Fear painted without asking

I drowned in you
Without asking
And it burned

I said thank you

Wine and Mothers (The Comedown)

My mother doesn't know
Where she went wrong with us all

She thinks
It was that sip of wine that night
Before the foetus was fully formed

She sits there and looks at me
Through the corner of her eye

And sighs
One of those long sighs that hold the world

She thinks
Of all the ways we could be better
But I can't

All my energy is recovering
From the sip of wine and her disappointment
In how things turned out

So she sips and turns away from here
Without those sighs
Drawing out the tide
Like warm sea air

Advice (Wise Contradictions)

Hearts are stupid.Brains are illogical.
Sugar's bad for you.Salt is too.Flour makes you
sneeze.
Don't play with white powders.

Listen to your brain.And your heart.And your gut.
They'll be wrong.

Play with fire.Fuck with alcohol.Blow shit up.
Burn your heart. Swallow so it burns.Swallow.
Don't be lazy.Be patient.Be calm.Fight for what you
want.Be still.

Have lots of sex. Don't have any sex. Sex is bad for
you.You'll die.Or like it.Or like the person.Or like
yourself.Or hate your thighs.Or fall in love.Or fall in
fuck.Or fall in a hole.Or fuck your fuck.Don't do that
shit.

You should just blow shit up.Find
enlightenment.Give it all up.
Or snort cocaine.

Bruises

12

There's a galaxy under your skin
You showed me peaks of rings
Your version of Saturn by accident

They came through a bit
When we were sleeping

Heads and limbs relaxed
To let in the Milky Way

Morning Exchange (Empty Prayer)

13

Sometimes I ask the day to be kind, to allow me to
melt into mornings like butter or your hands

He told me he does the same but they're hard for him
There's stiffness and pressure, and he fears the
chemicals,
How they could take over if he lets them in

I want to soften them for you, to carry you to
afternoons
When the sun can start its work

Let me take some weight,
Put it in my hands,
Until we're even

Universe

Earth tilts. If he was a bench the marble would fall.
Earth tilts. The liquid is slightly higher over there…
See? Just that side. Earth tilts. Left arm feels funny…
just a little, not always. Heart attack? Uneven time
zones make things better. It's midnight for him.
Maybe a little worse. Earth's unstable. He's a mess.
You want him but he's poison. You want her but she's
honey – you're allergic. Plastic toys slide to the
corners of the room as Earth tilts. It's shifting... now
they can't reach. The tilt gets larger but somehow you
don't notice. What axis? We're flat. Earth crumbles to
nothing. Your neighbourhood falls off the edge of the
universe. Earth's flat today, poor thing. You make tea,
argue over groceries. Earth tilts.

Moon pulls. Me to you. Hot to cinder. Melt to honey.
Ins to outs. Tides to currents to days to sand to shells
to molluscs to barbecue seafood dinners on the porch.
To courtyards and cacti in plastic tombs. Moon
watches. Pulls tides close. Moon, in the dark of night
when chests are open, tells the tales of the sea and
pours them in you. Watches you drown. Moon has
phases, no apologies. Slivers eternities in the ocean as
if not moving. You look for your keys. You laugh
about sadness. You drink wine to forget. You look up
one night. Moon pulls and you feel it in that moment.
It hits you and it hurts and you freeze and you choke.
Moon pulls.

Sun warms. Gives you grief if you want it. Blisters
on chests, angers on your faces. Paints them on, you
three-sided, two-faced mother-fucker. Heat you, free
you, burns liquids in you. My toes are cold. Sun
warms. Feels pain. Flicks rays to a gun of hatred and
pride. Baked heart caked on sourdough, crispy and
warm. Crack me. Too warm fuck off. Push away, find
shade, bake pie with a head in the oven. Sunburn. Go
away, come melt me, yes melt me, make me feel
something. I want you. Warm me. Sun warms –
fucking melt me fill me cut me open and sear me to
golden. I wish I was golden. Touch me but mean it.
Sun warms, then kills. Plays guitar when she can.
Wants to learn the keyboard, takes her mind off it all.
Drinks a mimosa. Calloused fingers strum hard. Kills
you, she kills you. Let me kill you. It hurts but you
eat it. You fucking eat me. Kill me. Sun warms.

A Nice Day

The cliff opened its mouth and let us in its throat
pools of clear saliva enticing and full
froze bone
stole breath
but didn't swallow
so we took it back like gods
or demolition crew
chipping at the rocks,
mouth walls crumbling into chunks in salted hands –
perpetrators
soaked in sun, our skin cooled and heated
cooled and heated
and we held the stones like kids
admiring destruction
or something of the sort
and threw them for fun
talking about how we too were crumbing beings
and it felt good, taking back control in that tiny way
as we walked across rocks doing just the same

Weekend Light

Morning weekend light draws rituals of coffee and
sesame seeds through his hands and feet

Fresh bread, the woman says thank you, sifts nods
our way in flour

As the sun comes out things are stiller than normal
With pauses and ritual hums beating each concrete
crevice

He tells me he can feel them all breathe out
Some communal agreement pulsing through their
arteries
Asleep in peace's womb

'Yes, things are alright, aren't they?'
A collective unison prayer for better days
He traces on me in braille

Flowers

He drew me a bunch of flowers
Sketched on a purple bow

Took me to the store
To spray perfume on each one

Said it'll be our way of playing God
But only the fun parts of the job

Family

19

Today I text my father
And told him I haven't been doing well
He didn't tell me
That his sister's on holiday in Budapest
Because she's dying
She'll be dead soon
He didn't answer
I asked my mother what she did for her birthday
She said she'd been asleep all day
I could hear her smoking through the phone
She said she feels old today
My sister doesn't speak to me
But I don't speak to her
So who's fault is that
As shared blood dries

On the Decay of Writing

Perhaps poetry is getting old because its message is
never clear
and sad things aren't always pretty
and no one's straight forward these days
and we're tired of reading fancy words
like love
or perhaps

Maybe words are tired
and we can't see what they make
inside our brains and heads
because we're tired
so we sit by ourselves
waiting for answers
or more distractions to keep us
feeling less empty and less alone
less ourselves

The Eucalypts (To a Future that Never Existed Between Us)

It's the future today
and suddenly we are old
having somehow made it through the ruddy haze of
tomorrow
to sit on a porch in Queensland's December.
We are sticky with the haze from our sweat and our
pasts
as you look at me and tell me your watch has stopped
the counter's clicked and
you're Tired
the T a capital, tall with meaning.

Your voice, clean and calm,
spits crisp words but don't make the distance –
they hover in the heat
and are swallowed by a blowfly.
I swat it away
kicking the screen door and leaving you there,
as if our porch is only yours and the words are your
pests,
thick and wet and crawling on the ground,
chooks pecking round your feet as you cluck back
telling them to eat until they're bursting

I swat you away now, picking arguments like a child -

we haven't painted the shed yet,

you want it blue and I yellow,
a stalemate to revisit tomorrow
until there isn't one

It's the future, or not, and my knuckles swell here
from all the things unsaid between us.
I make you tea each morning and do the same now,
watching as my hands ache from old,
holding words I can't express until they break open
and flow like the Condamine
and I drown in them
but only after feeding you tea,
hand to mouth, hand to mouth, careful not to drip
anything
or tell you I'll miss you

The screen door gives you shadows your face doesn't
hold.
I watch you as the kettle boils
your wrinkles sink deeper
your pale white beard reflecting the soft rolling
clouds
and I see you
but now is not the time for beauty.

How strange it is to want the end on a day like today,
so calm and so ordinary, The Eucalypts whispering as
they always do
while your tea turns the colour of tree bark and I
make you your toast.
This is my love for you, I tell the bread,

asking the day to be kind, to help me melt into
mornings
like butter or your hands.
Those mornings without you are coming so soon
and I feel my knuckles clench harder
asking for control in the worn metal handle.

Today is the future, the epilogue between chapters
And I sit with you and see the life you have lived.
It is painted on your face and soon on the shed.
You tell me the mornings are hardest for you now –
there's stiffness and pressure, and you fear the
chemicals,
your body a shell that crumbles like stone.
I want to soften them for you,
to carry you to afternoons when the sun can start its
work
Until the day comes and the birds don't sing
And I am here with the chooks
Not you
So I paint the shed blue as The Eucalypts whisper
Their voices hurting my hands.

www.ingramcontent.com/pod-product-compliance
Lightning Source LLC
LaVergne TN
LVHW010023200726
843495LV00015B/1906